DREAM
A Collection of Inspirational Poetry

ZaLonya Allen, Ph.D.

All rights reserved.
Copyright © 2005 by ZaLonya Allen
No part of this book may be reproduced or transmitted
in any form without permission in writing from the publisher.

LCCN: 2005908813

Library of Congress Cataloging-in-Publication Data

ZaLonya Allen

Dream: A Collection of Inspirational Poetry / ZaLonya Allen

Poetry

ISBN 0-9773891-0-3

Printed in the United States by Morris Publishing
3212 East Highway 30
Kearney, NE 68847
1-800-650-7888

ACKNOWLEDGMENTS

First and foremost, thank God! My belief allowed me to walk by faith, not by sight. Thank you to Zelma Smith Dexter, Michael Goodin, Jeff Miller, Doug Massey, Bonnie Firby, Dr. Donald Amboyer, and Joyce Silagy. Thank you for all of the opportunities you gave me. I will never forget those who assisted me when I started this journey. Thank you to my father James, my mother Jennie, and my brothers, Zegary, Van, and Zermont. Van, what a blessing you have been. Thanks to my sister-in law Joyce and my nephew Jameson. I am thankful to everyone who has touched my life. Through every experience I learned something that made me a better, stronger person.

DEDICATION

This book is dedicated to my mother, Jennie Allen. I remember everything. I remember all of the times you sacrificed your own happiness for me. I remember all of the long days and nights we spent on the road, traveling from city to city. I remember all of the motherly advice and pep talks you gave me, but most of all I remember your loyalty. No matter what happened, no matter how bad things looked, no matter what anyone said, your love and support never wavered. Thank you for giving me your creative genes, thank you for supporting my dreams, and thank you for believing in me!

TABLE OF CONTENTS

PART ONE – DARE TO DREAM
DREAM	2
START DREAMING	3
ONE LOVE ONE DREAM	5
YOU WERE MEANT TO FLY	6
IS IT IN YOU	7
TODAY BEAUTIFUL	9
SUCCESS IS WITHIN REACH	10
NO REGRETS	12
DREAM DREAM DREAM	13

PART TWO – STORMS OF LIFE
STORMY DAY	16
TODAY IS MY DESTINY	17
KEEP TRYING	19
WHAT LIES INSIDE OF ME	20
DESPITE DISAPPOINTMENT	22
THE TEARS IN MY EYES	23
PART OF THE PROCESS	24
FAITH IN THE DARK	25
PERSISTENCE	27
ON THE THRESHOLD OF GREATNESS	28

PART THREE – INSPIRATION TIME
HE IS REAL	32
WHAT GOD HAS FOR YOU	33
DO YOU EVER	34
FAITH IS THE ANSWER	35
GUARDIAN ANGEL	36
THANK GOD FOR YOU	37
THIS IS MY CALLING	38
SPRING IN BLOOM	40
THE MYSTERY OF THE MASTER	41

PART FOUR – INTROSPECTION

THE DISTANCE BETWEEN SUCCESS AND FAILURE	44
A BATTLE AGAINST MYSELF	46
INVISIBLE CELL	47
INNER CHILD	48
POWERFUL PERSPECTIVE	50
ALONE WITH MY THOUGHTS	52
ME AND MY MAN	53
I WILL TELL YOU WHAT TO THINK OF ME	54

PART FIVE – AFTER THE STORM

AFTER THE RAIN	56
THE SUN IS SHINING IN MY WORLD	57
UNCONDITIONALLY YOU	58
THE BEAUTY OF A DREAM	59
AN AMAZING PLACE THROUGH CLEAR GLASSES	60
DISCOVERING HAPPINESS	61
YES I CAN	62
I DON'T KNOW WHY	63
STAND UP	64

PART SIX – MOTIVATIONS

STILL HERE STILL STANDING AND IN MY RIGHT MIND	66
THERE IS AN EAGLE IN YOU	68
THE LITTLE THINGS	69
GREATNESS IS YOUR DESTINY	70
A NEW DAY	71
GIVE IT TO YOURSELF	72
IMAGINATION	73
PRETENDING ON A BAD DAY	74
RARE	75

PART SEVEN – LOVE AND LIFE

DREAM LOVE	*78*
AN UNKNOWN LOVE	*79*
LOVE FROM A DISTANCE	*81*
COULD THIS BE LOVE THIS TIME	*82*
TRUE LOVE	*83*
EYES THAT SPEAK	*84*
OBSERVATION POINT	*85*
WHAT YOUR LOVE HAS DONE TO ME	*86*

PART EIGHT – SOCIAL AWARENESS

AT WAR	*88*
MAHOGANY SKIN	*90*
ILLEGAL SUBSTANCE	*92*
EVERYBODY IS SOMEBODY	*93*
THROUGH THE EYES OF A CHILD	*95*
YESTERDAY TODAY AND TOMORROW	*96*
THE POWER OF ONE	*98*

INTRODUCTION

This book is meant to motivate, inspire, and provoke thought in the mind of the reader. It is a self-help poetry book. The content represents both real and fictional accounts of serious issues facing our society today including domestic violence, substance abuse, self-esteem, and spirituality. As you read these words you may recall some of your own personal experiences. You may get a new idea or be moved to action; but I believe one thing for sure, after reading this book, you will never be the same. Someone once said, "Once the mind has been expanded by a new thought it never returns to its former dimensions." When we are born we have no preconceived ideas about life. Experience teaches us most of what we know. As children many of us dream of doing the impossible, of flying the way birds fly or possessing super powers like superman, until reality convinces us of how ridiculous it is to dream. Not only do we stop dreaming of the impossible, but many of us stop dreaming of what is possible. I encourage you to give yourself permission to dream and then follow those dreams wherever they may lead you.

Part One
Dare to Dream

DREAM

Dream the grandest dreams
you can think of,
make them as limitless
as the sky above,
don't worry about if and
when they will come true,
have faith and let the
divine light lead you.

START DREAMING

When you dream big dreams
people will tell you to stop.
Be a realist, they say,
you'll never reach the top.

People laughed at my dreams
and made me cry.
At times I was tempted
to kiss my dreams goodbye.

But still I dreamt
of living a wonderful life,
in spite of the pain
that cut deep like a knife.

I believed that one day
the sun would shine
and on that day
victory would be mine.

When they tell you to stop
you have to be strong.
Don't let anyone convince you
that having a dream is wrong.

It seems society encourages
us to keep it real,
get a job, pay bills,
and become run of the mill.

But I say start dreaming
before it's too late,
while you still have a
chance don't hesitate.

Start dreaming because the
world is full of possibility
and if you want a part of it
you have to take responsibility.

Start dreaming even
if it puts you in a lonely place.
Sometimes in life you just
have to run your own race.

Start dreaming and
no matter what you do,
never stop dreaming
because dreams do come true.

ONE LOVE ONE DREAM
By Jennie Allen and ZaLonya Allen

One love, one dream
to always pursue,
what a beautiful theme,
not for everyone but for you.

As long as there is life,
through storm, rain and strife,
keep believing, keep trying,
sometimes laughing and sometimes crying,

and one day it will come,
that dream will be done
and the battle will be won.

No matter how impossible it may seem,
never give up on your dream.

YOU WERE MEANT TO FLY

We were all meant to fly,
much like the eagles in the sky,
but we must soar in our own special way,
with the gifts God gave us on our birthday.

We all have talents lying deep within
but too often we fail to begin.

We give in to insecurity and doubt,
burying our dreams so they can't get out,
and then obstacles get in the way
and it hurts more than words can say.

Inside you feel something dying,
sometimes you feel tired of trying.

Bearing the intensity of your own private storm,
you think your suffering is different from the norm.
Pain is something many go through
but whether you survive or not is up to you.

Never give in to thoughts of defeat
because determination can never be beat.

There is strength inside each of us
but perseverance is a must,
so always set your sights high
because you, with your gifts, were meant to fly.

IS IT IN YOU

Is it in you
To make your dreams come true,
To step out on faith and try something new,
To taste the bitter with the sweet,
To keep bouncing back from failure and defeat?

Is it in you
To take a risk, not knowing the outcome,
To believe that something great is what you'll become,
To laugh when you want to cry,
To get up and give it one more try?

Is it in you
To feel alone and misunderstood,
To believe in yourself the way you should,
To be strong when things go wrong,
To believe the pain won't last for long?

Is it in you
To question everything you believe in,
To have your faith tested again and again,
To stay up tossing and turning all night,
To hold on to faith with all your might?

Is it in you
To have your family look at you shaking their head,
To have them think you are crazy or misled,
To get to a point where you question your own sanity,
To wonder if you really are chasing a fantasy?

Is it in you
To be brave when fear has overcome you,
To be courageous and do what you must do,
To endure in the eye of the storm,
To become you in your greatest form?

Is it in you
To hear "no" when you want to hear "yes",
To believe you are destined for greatness and to accept no less,
To persevere and never say die,
To know until your last breath you're going to try?

Is it in you
To be stubborn, bold and daring,
To let people whisper and talk without caring,
To develop a vision in your mind's eye,
To hold that vision and never let it die?

Is it in you
To see the sun when others see clouds,
To know that one day you will make mama proud,
To give all that you have to give,
To celebrate life and let your dreams live?

Is it in you
To reach down deep into your soul,
To pull out the strength to reach your goal,
To climb that last mountain to reach the top,
Or will life's obstacles convince you to stop?

It is in you
To do all of these things and more
Because like the eagles you were meant to soar.
It is in you!

TODAY BEAUTIFUL

Today is going to be a beautiful day
because I have decided to make it that way.

I can be negative if I choose to be
or I can focus on all the positive that I see.

There is so much I can be grateful for
and so much more for me to explore.

Sadness is no longer an option for me,
realizing that I have choices is the key.

I have faith that many good things lay ahead
but I can't allow my heart or mind to be misled.

Tomorrow can be beautiful too,
especially when you know what to do.

Choose a smile instead of a frown
and cease feeling down.

Choose the sun over the rain
and let its rays chase away the pain.

Choose to spread love instead of hate
and let happiness be your fate.

Choose to be happy no matter what
and don't waste one precious day in a rut.

SUCCESS IS WITHIN REACH

Success is what happens
when you reach your goal,
giving all you have to give,
your mind, body, and soul.

It's the result of relentless effort,
hard work and determination,
it's believing that one day you
will reach your destination.

Success is something
that we all desire,
to live our dreams so we
keep reaching higher.

When you say you have dreams
some people just laugh,
but don't let that discourage you, for
in life we must choose our own path.

Sure there will be challenges to face
but victories to embrace.
There will be mountains to climb,
races against time.

No it won't be easy, there will
be many obstacles to overcome,
you see the road to success is
not for everyone, just some.

It's for those who are willing
to endure the pain, and the rain
and to make sacrifices
for every gain.

It's for those who are willing to
believe that tomorrow will be brighter
and say "I won't give up
because I'm a fighter."

Always remember, your wants, your dreams,
your deepest desires, are yours to keep,
but in order to achieve, you must believe
success is within reach.

NO REGRETS

Live today like there is no tomorrow,
give everything that you have inside.

Don't worry about what anyone thinks,
people have been talking for a while.

Keep your focus on the things you want,
you are bound to reach your goals.

Live life to the fullest today
and tomorrow there will be no regrets.

What a reward to know you gave life your all,
blood, sweat and tears.

What a reward to end your life your way,
happy, peaceful, and content.

What a reward to never have to say,
would've, should've, could've.

Live life to the fullest today,
and tomorrow there will be no regrets.

DREAM DREAM DREAM

When your dreams seem so far away
And you feel as though you can't live them today
Close your eyes and slip away
To a place where you can have your way.

Imagine the life you've dreamt about
And in this moment release all doubt.

Go ahead and walk right into your dream
Never mind how unreal it may initially seem.
Create vivid images careful and slow
Relax and go anywhere you dare to go.

DREAM DREAM DREAM.

See every color you are supposed to see.
Make them as bright and vivid as can be.
Smell every scent that might be around,
And don't forget to include the sound.

Feel everything you need to feel.
Do your best to make this dream seem real.

Smell the freshness of the air you breathe,
And just remember you must believe.
Get in the middle of what you're dreaming about,
Now sit back and watch your dream play out.

DREAM DREAM DREAM.

Now open your eyes and come back and know
That you can go there any time you want to go.
Where you are free to be what you want to be.
Where you are free to see what you want to see.

Instead of letting reality make you sad,
Experience in your mind what you want so bad.

One day your dreams won't only be in your mind,
They will be here in the physical in due time.
But until that wonderful and glorious day,
Don't let anyone take your dreams away.

DREAM DREAM DREAM.

Part Two
Storms of Life

STORMY DAY

I drifted off to sleep late last night
After struggling through a day that wasn't quite right.

Thinking of the ills people warned me about,
Soon I was overcome with fear and doubt.

I worried about life flashing before my eyes,
Suddenly chasing dreams didn't seem so wise.

People said it was foolish to chase pie in the sky
But I didn't listen, I continued to try.

Now I lay awake in the middle of the night,
Empty promises, broken dreams and no end in sight.

Today represents a storm in my life,
How I long for an end to pain and strife.

It is natural to have these feelings every now and then
But each time you fall you must get up again.

During the storms you find out who you really are.
Will you be a quitter or emerge as a rising star?

Most people don't make it because they give in.
We must learn to gather reserved strength from within.

It is a strength that abides in each of us,
An abundance of power you can call on when you must.

Stormy days don't last forever,
So don't succumb in inclement weather.

If you can believe things will work out fine,
Like a diamond in the rough you'll shine in time.

TODAY IS MY DESTINY

I am at the place and time in my
life where I am supposed to be.
Everything that I have experienced
up to this point is what made me.

Today is my destiny.

Now is the time for me to
reflect on the past.
Surpass painful memories
and make the good ones last.

However I must recall all
experiences in totality
for there is much to be learned
from even my harshest reality.

Today is my destiny.

I have had experiences
that shake the soul,
makes one numb and helps
the spirit grow cold.

How can I escape the memories
that keep haunting me?
Sometimes I want to run
to a place where I won't be.

There's no escaping yourself,
everywhere you go, there you are.
You can try to run but you
won't get very far.

You just have to be still and
deal with your stuff.
Brace yourself because it's
going to be tough.

From the depths of pain
arises strength and wisdom.
Take comfort in knowing there
is refuge in God's kingdom

Today is my destiny.

KEEP TRYING

When the storms of life are raging out of control
And you're on the verge of abandoning your goal
Keep Trying.

When your money is insufficient
And internally you're feeling deficient
Keep Trying.

When people snub you for no reason at all
And everywhere you turn you hit the wall
Keep Trying.

When the people you love disappoint you
And you're asking our father to anoint you
Keep Trying.

When fear has its arms around you
And you can't do the things you want to do
Keep Trying.

When sickness seems to be having its way
And you wonder how you'll make it through the day
Keep trying.

When you feel like giving up, you must resist.
Victory only comes to those who persist.
Keep trying.

WHAT LIES INSIDE OF ME

People look at my exterior
and jump to conclusions.
Appearances are sometimes
just an illusion.

"You can't do it"
is what they like to say.
I just ignore them
and do it anyway.

People tell me
I won't make it,
that I'm not strong
enough to take it.

But they don't know what's inside of me

People say I don't look
like what I want to be,
but who are they
to judge me?

I have dreams as big
and grand as the sky,
and it's just a matter of time
before I fly.

Some laugh when they hear
what I want to do.
They don't believe
my dreams will come true.

But they don't know what's inside of me.

Inside of me
dwell my own convictions.
on which I refuse to
put any restrictions.

Inside of me
is a heart unwilling to compromise,
only heightened by those
anxious for my demise.

Inside of me
there is a temple,
a holy place where
life is made simple.

Inside of me
there is a divine presence
which identifies me
and defines my essence.

Inside of me lives
the spirit of God,
therefore all things
are possible no matter how odd.

DESPITE DISAPPOINTMENT

Today I feel disappointed
As I learn that what I want will never happen.
I am struggling to find something positive to hold on to.

Today I feel empty
As I experience the loss of what I wanted so badly.
I am agonizing over the permanency of this situation.

Today I feel numb
As I ponder over the lessons I have been forced to learn.
I am looking for answers to all the questions in my mind.

Today I feel determined
As I decide that I can't let this consume me.
I am finding the strength to go on and be all that I can be.

Today I feel tenacious
As I continue to pursue my purpose in life.
I am not going to let today stand in my way.

Today I feel encouraged
As I explore a multitude of mixed emotions.
I am persevering despite the disappointment I feel today.

THE TEARS IN MY EYES

The tears in my eyes
reflect the feelings of an
introvert so painfully shy.

They come when I laugh
they come when I cry
they come when I feel
I don't want to try.

Some days I feel up and
want to soar to the sky.
Some days I feel down
And don't know how I'll get by.

People like to talk about you
and tell you what you
should and shouldn't do
but no one knows of the memories,
the pain, the shame, the insecurities,
the feelings way down deep inside
the feelings I tried hard to hide.

So the tears in my eyes
will come and go
reflecting those times
when I feel high and low.

Until the day I can look
through the tears
and become brave enough to
face down my fears.

PART OF THE PROCESS

Everyone can have a dream, it doesn't cost a dime
Just a little hard work and a whole lot of time,
But it's tough when doors are slammed in your face
And everyone seems to be on your case,
Criticizing everything you do
And trampling over your dreams too.

Remember the vision can become a reality
And that challenges are just a formality.

Pain is part of the process you must go through
Getting through it is all up to you.
When all you want to do is cry
And you find yourself asking the Lord why
Never forget that you are worthy of the best
And in your darkest hour you will be put to the test.

FAITH IN THE DARK

As night falls, darkness
looms outside my window.
I can't remember the
last time I felt this low.

Will all of the sacrificing
I did ever pay off,
and what about my hardened
heart that used to be so soft?

I want my heart back filled
with the love that used to be there
and free of the pain that so
many of us seem to share.

I long to smile from my joy
and to laugh from my heart.
I want to recapture the life in
my spirit that has fallen apart.

Instead my face is inundated
with fake expressions of joy.
Why must we play with our
emotions like a childhood toy?

Right now life is a battle that
I'm fighting through each day,
But while I'm lost in darkness
my faith leads the way.

I just keep telling myself,
walk by faith, not by sight
Live your life
with all your might.

In desperate times
faith is all you have.
I have faith it will be
All right in the aftermath.

PERSISTENCE

If you feel tired, you can't give up.
If you feel beaten, it's time to get tough.

You have a dream that problems can't interrupt.
You have to hold on when things get rough.

You may get sick with an unexpected disease.
You may find your confidence under siege.

You may lose some of your family and friends.
You may even feel discouraged when it ends.

You may run out of money.
You may find loved ones acting funny.

You may be snubbed for no reason at all.
You may find some waiting for your fall.

Remember that only the strong can survive.
So persevere and keep your dreams alive.

ON THE THRESHOLD OF GREATNESS

When your journey has you
down and running out of energy
instead of giving up, find a way
to create some synergy.

Join together with those who are
traveling along the same path.
Together you can accomplish
the most difficult of tasks.

The road to success is full of twists,
turns, obstacles and more.
The path won't be straight,
it will be filled with detours.

And like a soldier returning
from the battlefields,
weary but optimistic because
your spirit wasn't killed.

You must somehow regain the
enthusiasm you once had,
although all of the challenges
have you feeling bad.

Have you noticed the storm is
raging stronger than it ever has?
That's because your hopes and
dreams are about to come to pass.

Everything you've ever wanted
is about to arrive.
Hold on a little while longer
because you can survive.

You are on the threshold of greatness
with dreams about to come true.
Don't give up because you're about to
experience a world prosperous and new.

Part Three
Inspiration Time

HE IS REAL

Some believe that there is no God
I find that reasoning rather odd.

If one has questions I can understand
Because no one knows God's plan.

But to say that he does not exist
Is completely illogical, I must insist.

Confusion is something one may feel
But life is proof that he is real.

Who created the spirit that resides in you?
Who gave you the strength to do what you do?

Who put birds in the sky and fish in the sea?
Who unconditionally accepts and loves you and me?

Who brilliantly placed the flowers and the trees?
Who could've invented a warm summer breeze?

Who made the ocean so mystical and blue?
Who answers prayer and makes dreams come true?

The Almighty is the answer to this question.
Think and you may make this confession.

God can perform the most remarkable of tasks.
To get your blessings all you have to do is ask.

Accept him into your life and let your heart heal,
All you need to do is proclaim that he is real.

WHAT GOD HAS FOR YOU

Don't worry about what the evil do.
No man can take what God has for you.

Listen to what he speaks into your heart
And don't be afraid to make a new start.

Trust in him, he will never let you down.
He will be your friend when no one is around.

Even when you can't see a way out
And everyone around you is filled with doubt.

When nothing seems to make any sense,
Life is out of control and the storm is intense

Just remember during your darkest hour
The Almighty God has the ultimate power.

He did not bring you this far to leave you.
Ask and then listen, he will lead you.

So don't worry about what the evil do
Because no man can take what God has for you.

DO YOU EVER

Do you ever question the meaning of your existence,
Feeling like somehow you could make a difference?

Do you ever wonder why you are here,
Experiencing feelings of love, hate and fear?

Do you ever wonder what tomorrow will bring,
Hoping for a reason to dance or a reason to sing?

Do you ever wonder where people go when they die,
If there's really a heaven or if that's just a lie?

Do you ever wonder how planes stay in the sky,
Flying amongst the eagles thousands of feet high?

Do you ever feel sad and alone,
Even among friends where you're loved and well known?

Do you ever wonder why some have more than enough,
While some have always had it rough?

Do you ever wonder why relationships don't last,
And why people fall in and out of love so fast?

Do you ever question the purpose of tomorrow,
Hoping it will be a day filled with joy, not sorrow?

Do you ever wonder if God hears your prayers,
Waiting for a sign to let you know that he cares?

FAITH IS THE ANSWER

My heart is heavy with many burdens to bear.
This journey has taught me life is not fair.

My eyes have grown tired of shedding meaningless tears.
Crying does nothing to solve problems and fears.

I'm feeling lost in a daze not knowing what to believe.
Entertaining every negative thought my mind can conceive.

So much has gone wrong I forget what has gone right
It seems life has become one long sleepless night.

When you get discouraged how do you go on,
When all hope is lost and ambition has gone?

Faith is the answer to such a critical question.
It is where you can turn for strength and direction.

Put a smile on your face and a twinkle in your eye,
And then pick yourself up and give it one more try.

You have not been forsaken; you are too precious for that.
Your faith is being tested and that is the fact.

Put your faith where you know it belongs.
Trust in him even when everything has gone wrong.

Be still and believe things are going to get better.
And like the pieces to a puzzle, it will all come together.

GUARDIAN ANGEL

I have a guardian angel,

An angel that watches over me
And keeps me out of harm's way
Guiding me down the right
Paths and safely through each day.

I am a spiritual being searching
To make sense of each day
But every now and then, the
Unexpected comes my way.

On days when I am struggling for
A reason to be conscious,
A reason to be concerned,
A reason to be in this world,
A reason yet to be learned,
I remember my guardian angel.

The angel that watches over me
When I have lost my direction,
Helping me to understand the
Meaning of her love and protection.

If it doesn't kill you it will make
You stronger, someone once said,
Words of wisdom that should
Remain in the heart and head.

From my experiences I gain strength
To rise from beneath the ruins,
To rise to any occasion,
To rise to this new day,
To rise from my abrasions.

I have a guardian angel.

THANK GOD FOR YOU

One day I imagined a world without you.
I soon realized, a world without you would be blue.
Suddenly I felt lost and without a clue
because without you I wouldn't know what to do.

Thank God for you.

You are my sunshine on a cloudy day,
a beacon of light when darkness falls and I lose my way.
You are the eyes that help me see,
you are my shield when people throw rocks at me.

Thank God for you.

I look to you when I want to be strong,
because with you the weak cannot last long.
I won't give up, for you give me the will to live,
because of the love you so graciously give.

Thank God for you.

Never again will I imagine a world without you
because without you I wouldn't know what to do.
No matter how far I roam you will remain with me.
Forever in my heart is where you will to be.

THIS IS MY CALLING

Tears flowed down my cheeks tonight,
Like a steady stream triggered by fright.

Things aren't going the way I planned
And the pressure is more than I can stand.

Confused, I questioned the direction of my life,
Then I realized I was called to speak and write.

This is my calling.

In my spirit I feel this is what I was meant to do,
Touch the lives of those battered and bruised.

Whenever I try to walk away
My heart won't let my mind go astray.

A divine force pulls me back in
And I'm on the roller coaster ride again.

This is my calling.

When you get the call there is something you must do,
Answer the call and to thy own self be true.

Pursue your calling with everything in you,
Do not discard what you were sent to do.

Each of us is called to do something in life,
I was called to speak and write.

This is my calling.

There is something you were meant to do.
What is it that is uniquely you?

You owe it to the world to share your gift,
But you may need to make a mental shift.

Although the journey can be trying at times,
Listen to what's in your heart and mind.

This is your calling.

SPRING IN BLOOM

Spring is like a song to me,
When all the world sings a melody.

It's an array of flowers in bloom,
An abundance of beauty to consume.

Colors so bold to behold,
The elements of a mystery unfold.

A gust of wind creates a gentle breeze,
An invisible force moving through the trees.

From mountains so high to valleys so low,
To deep blue waters where clear rivers flow.

A world given life by the breath of the sun,
When heaven and earth become one.

And then day gives way to night,
Giving birth to an awesome sight.

It comes with a calm that soothes the soul
And harbors secrets better left untold.

A magical evening about to unfurl,
As the moon illuminates throughout the world.

Stars like diamonds span the sky,
Sparking above the world so high.

Spring, the grandest of all seasons.
A celebration of life for many reasons.

THE MYSTERY OF THE MASTER

Life is a mystery to me.
It has a rationale many fail to see.

Why does the sun go up and down?
Why does the earth spin around and around?

Why do the seasons constantly change?
Why do we experience joy and pain?

It is the mystery of the master.

Where and why did it all begin?
When and how will it all end?

This life, this world, I don't understand.
What is the purpose, what is the master plan?

Some say the mystery will be revealed in the end.
These questions will linger on until then.

Part Four
Introspection

THE DISTANCE BETWEEN SUCCESS AND FAILURE

Look at who you are and think
about who you would like to become.
How are you going to merge the
two visions of yourself into one?
First you have to figure out where
your insecurities come from.

The distance between what is
and what could be lies in our fears.
Consider the faulty information
learned during your formative years,
and reflect on the inner turmoil
that often has you close to tears.

Too much of what we accept as
true is either unrealistic or illogical.
We must not give weight to that
which is negative and diabolical.
Follow your heart because
dreams don't have to be methodical.

In your quest for peace and happiness
work from the inside out.
Look within when attempting to
figure out what your life is all about.
The secret lies in resisting giving
in to insecurity, fear and doubt.

The vision you hold for
yourself can be made real.
Uncover your wounds, treat them,
and then allow them to heal.
Don't run from the pain that
you inevitably have to feel.

The distance between success and
failure varies from one person to another.
The length and depth of your
journey to this place is yours to uncover.
Remember that the peace that comes
from self-acceptance is like no other.

A BATTLE AGAINST MYSELF

I am fighting the battle against myself today.
There are two sides to me and each one wants her way.

The positive side always has something good to say.
The negative side spouts doubt and confusion all day.

A negative voice is there to remind me of what could go wrong.
A positive voice tells me it's all possible if I just stay strong.

We often look externally when life isn't what we want it to be.
I looked internally when I realized my greatest obstacle was me.

It is the negative internal dialogue that goes on all the time.
And the questions in my head reeking havoc on my mind.

It is the choice to allow negative comments to affect me.
It is cautiously treading through life too carefully.

One must believe in oneself, leaving no room for doubt.
One must hold nothing back, allowing gifts to play full out.

One must be able to withstand pressure, heartache and pain.
One must be able to stand up to life's fury and rain.

Listen to the things you tell yourself all the time,
Is it moving you forward or devastating your mind?

When you want to try something new a battle rages within.
And you don't always know whether to fight or give in.

Who can be sure of every thing every time?
There may be some doubt in the back of your mind.

Prepare to fight anything negative that gets in your way,
Even if it is you, disregard what the negative self may say.

INVISBLE CELL

I have to break through the walls that bind me.
There is an invisible cell that seeks to confine me.

My mind put me in a cell and threw away the key.
It is a reality many of us fail to see.

We place the limits on ourselves,
Allowing our dreams to sit on the shelves.

But how can we now break free,
When we don't know any other way to be.

We have to change the way we think,
Our internal and external worlds are forever linked.

If I think I am a failure then that is all I can be.
If I think I am a winner I will see a new me.

We are all controlled by the thoughts in our mind.
Fill your mind with thoughts of a different kind.

Like a volcano of potential about to erupt,
Change the way you think and watch your world open up.

INNER CHILD

Inside each of us there is an inner child
The child you have not acknowledged in a while

The one who stumbled trying to learn how to walk
The one who stuttered trying to learn how to talk.

The one who cried for candy and ice cream,
The one who couldn't sleep after a bad dream

The one who was afraid on the first day of school
The one who couldn't seem to follow the rules

The one who got picked on and teased everyday
The one who felt inadequate in every way

The one who often felt abandoned and alone
The one who woke up today full grown.

That inner child still lives in each of us.
Acknowledging her presence is a must.

You are forever connected to the child in you.
As an adult that child affects everything you do.

Think about the adult you've become
The one who seeks approval from everyone

The one who feels unloved and misunderstood
The one who was told, "you're no good"

The one who is so afraid of rejection
The one who seeks love and affection

The one who finds fault with everyone
The one who is emotionally on the run

The one who overindulges to escape from pain
The one who can't deal with guilt, hurt and shame

The one who blames everybody for everything
The one who doesn't understand the joy she could bring

The one who smiles when close to tears
The one who denies problems and fears.

When you completely accept yourself
You will experience spiritual wealth.

Acknowledge the inner child in you
Give her the love that is long overdue.

Embrace her in your arms and seal it with a kiss
Just to be loved is her only true wish.

To yourself unconditional love is the gift you must give
To experience the life you were meant to live.

POWERFUL PERSPECTIVE

The way you experience life
is dependent upon your perspective.
However, the window through which you
view the world can often be deceptive.

Especially if your vision is clouded
with memories from a jaded past.
Bad experiences tend to occupy the mind,
pierce the heart and last and last.

Out of repeated failure, disappointment
and pain a pessimist is born,
spending countless hours awaiting
unexpected reasons to mourn.

Is the glass half empty or is it
half full is an age old question.
The answer you give can provide
a glimpse into your life's direction.

At any given moment you can choose
to seek the light or slip into darkness.
The power is in realizing you don't have
to live a life grounded in harshness.

When you feel like crying
you can choose laughter over tears.
A positive attitude will strengthen
your soul and dissipate your fears.

We get what we expect because
we subconsciously seek it out.
Your perspective is what determines
what your life is all about.

Become an eternal optimist
and anticipate a favorable outcome.
When you believe in possibilities
there's no limit to what you can become.

ALONE WITH MY THOUGHTS

Today I want to be alone with my thoughts,

The thoughts that run through my mind when no one is around,
The thoughts that relax me and restore my soul,
The thoughts that make me uncomfortable and challenge me,
The thoughts about my victories that put a smile on my face,
The thoughts about my trials that put a tear in my eye,
The thoughts about my greatest hopes and dreams for the future,
The thoughts about questions and feelings I can't explain,
The thoughts that shape my character and define who I am.

Today I want to be alone with my thoughts,

So that I can see where I have been,
So that I will know where I am going,
So that I can learn from my mistakes,
So that I can understand myself better,
So that I can discover who I want to become,
So that I can enjoy the journey to my destination,
So that I can experience tranquility and peace,
So that I can be who I was meant to be.

Today I want to be alone with my thoughts.

ME AND MY MAN

He hit me again and he said he wouldn't do that
Now I'm walking around in sunglasses and a big hat.

I am tired of wearing this ridiculous disguise,
Hoping no one will notice me and my black eyes.

How can I love someone who hurts me this way?
Risking my life for love is a high price to pay.

Especially when it ain't love between me and my man,
Not when he keeps hitting me with the back of his hand.

So why won't I leave if I know something's wrong?
It's because of what we've been taught for far too long.

A woman ain't much without a man by her side,
So when he does wrong, just let it slide.

I guess I believe it because I'm still here,
And when I think about leaving, all I feel is fear.

At least I know my self-worth is not where it should be
And I know that I am the only one who can save me.

I WILL TELL YOU WHAT TO THINK OF ME

What you think of me is a
reflection of what I think of myself.
It is in direct proportion to
my physical and mental health.

I tell you what to think
of me by the way I walk.
I tell you what to think
of me by the way I talk.

You will respect me
if I demand that you do.
If I believe that I am special
then you might too.

If I let you yell at me
and tell me I am no good,
Would you do it again
just because you knew you could?

If I smile at you
perhaps you'll say hello or have a great day.
If I frown at you
perhaps you'll ignore me and turn away.

I wear the way I feel
like an article of clothing,
Whether it's love that I am feeling
or self-hatred and loathing.

You will respond to the
non-verbal cues that I am displaying,
and dance to the music coming
from the instrument I am playing.

Part Five
After the Storm

AFTER THE RAIN

After the rain there is sun
and that holds true for everyone.

After a storm there is a rainbow
that can be seen from anywhere you go.

After a dark night there is a bright day,
darkness never comes to stay.

After winter comes spring
and beautiful birds with a song to sing.

After death there is new life,
change comes but the spirit stays alive.

After somber moments comes cheer
so hold on, for lighter moments are near.

THE SUN IS SHINING IN MY WORLD

Although I can look outside and see clouds
the sun is shining in my world.
This morning I looked in the mirror and thought
"a new life is about to unfurl."

With so many reasons to sigh and few real reasons
to try, I put a smile on my face.
With so much wisdom in my mind and so much courage
in my heart, I have been blessed by God's grace.

At any moment in time we can really rejoice
about everything in life that is good.
We don't really take the time to focus our minds
on the positive the way that we should.

No matter how bleak the outlook may sometimes seem
you don't have to suffer through a cloudy day.
Let the sun shine in your life with each day you begin
and emerge in a confident way.

UNCONDITIONALLY YOU

Why do you worry about what others think of you,
carefully executing everything you say and do.

It is emotionally draining to live life this way,
making unnecessary adjustments from day to day.

You will never be able to please everyone,
regardless of the good works you've done.

Just be who you are, whatever the circumstances,
live life to the fullest and take your chances.

Love yourself unconditionally and feel free to be you
instead of watching everything you say and do.

Self-acceptance is every problem's solution,
soul searching will allow you to draw this conclusion.

And at the end of the day you can put your mind at ease
releasing your worries of those you tried to please.

THE BEAUTY OF A DREAM

A dream is a beautiful vision to hold,
a picture created in the mind of man.

Sunny days, blue skies, joy and laughter
can all be a part of the vision.

Add all the ideas your mind can conceive,
no limits, no hardships, no boundaries.

The potential in dreams lies in your heart's desire,
it's what your mind dares to imagine

Images of a life filled with happiness,
every need fulfilled, all wishes granted.

A dream can seem so illusive at times,
an intangible idea evolving.

But keep the faith and keep on trying,
breathe life into your dreams to keep them from dying.

AN AMAZING PLACE THROUGH CLEAR GLASSES

It's amazing how the sun can light up the world
Like a chandelier illuminating a room.

It's incredible how deep the blue rivers run
Like an eternal pool never ceasing.

It's astonishing how the wind blows with such strength
Like an invisible force exerting its power.

It's stunning how beautiful a flower can be
Like a piece of art work in a museum.

It's unbelievable how tall the trees can grow
Like a skyline designed by nature.

It's remarkable how the days continue to evolve
Like an endless circle of darkness and light.

It's awesome how stars spangle the night sky
Like a thousand jewels sparkling bright.

The world is an amazing place when
you look at it through clear glasses.

You'll see it when you look from a positive lens
on each day as it quickly passes.

DISCOVERING HAPPINESS

Happiness is a state of
being we all search for
but no matter how much we
get we seem to want more.

Some people think the answers
lie in material things
but limited joy is what
things can bring.

Some think finding a mate
will lead them to their goal
but to find true happiness
we must look within our soul.

So often we look outside of
ourselves for what we need
when an internal place is where
our search should lead.

Don't spend your life
searching without a clue
realize the answer to
happiness resides within you.

Happiness is your choice
make the choice to be happy.

YES I CAN

I can have it all,
withstand any test and overcome any wall.
In some of my attempts I may fall
but I will get up again and again and stand tall
because I know I can have it all.

Yes I can.

I can go to college and earn a degree.
I can be anything I want to be.

I can be a doctor or a lawyer or an engineer,
but I must work hard and be courageous in the face of fear.

I can overcome any obstacle that comes my way,
if I just let my conscious and good judgments lead the way.

Yes I can.

Some may doubt me but it doesn't matter what they say
because this belief in myself is here to stay.

I believe I can live in a mansion on a hill.
If I choose I can drive an exquisite automobile.

I have the power to control my destiny.
Once I make up my mind no one can stop me.

I can live the life of my dreams.
I can have it all no matter how impossible it seems.

Yes I can.

I DON'T KNOW WHY

Chaos is the state of mind I'm in.
Sometimes it seems impossible to win.

Yet winning is all I can think about
but in the back of my mind there is some doubt.

Chasing dreams has been the hardest thing I've ever done.
It has been like a test to see how fast I can run.

Will I fail or will I succeed?
Faith in things unseen is what I need.

All I can think about are these dreams of mine
in a world where reality can be so unkind.

When life gets tough I will continue to try
because I can't give up and I don't know why.

STAND UP

There are things that I want
and my patience is running out.
Up until now I thought I understood
what life was about.

You choose what you want
and pursue it with all of your heart,
but some-where along the way
that plan fell apart.

Sometimes the things we want
take longer than we planned
and instead of giving up
you have to take a stand.

Stand up for the dreams that
you've been fighting so hard to achieve.
Stand up against adversity
even if you are the only one who believes.

Stand up when you are tired
and think you can't take any more.
Stand up and keep knocking
on opportunity's closed door.

Stand up for all those who had
dreams but eventually gave in.
Stand up and show the world that
with determination you can win.

Stand up and let the faith that
brought you this far carry you home.
Stand up and know that you are
not walking this journey alone.

Part Six
Motivations

STILL HERE STILL STANDING
AND IN MY RIGHT MIND

When I think about all that has happened to me
I thank God that I am still here, still standing
and in my right mind.

The days have been hard and the nights have been long,
the disappointments have been many.
At times I felt my mind drifting to distant places.

Through it all I had to believe
that something better was in store for me.
I had to believe that there was a plan for my life and
that everything that happened to me happened for a reason
and that my hurt would only last for a season.

The things that did not kill me made me stronger.
Painful experiences helped me to understand others' suffering.
I constantly had to ask myself,
"What can I learn from this experience?"
"How can I use this experience to help someone else?"

The most important lesson I learned was that
no matter how tough things got,
no matter how many times I got knocked down,
no matter how badly someone talked about me,
no matter how many lies had been told,
no matter how much pain I was feeling,
no matter how much I wanted to give up,

I had to keep fighting.
I had to fight jealousy and envy.
I had to fight hatred and fear.
I had to fight guilt and shame.
I had to look evil in the eye and yell, "I'm not backing down."
I had to get up from the ground over and over again.
I had to love myself enough to make my dreams come true.

My desire was stronger than my fear.
My determination was more resilient than my pain.
My will to win was more fierce than any man's contempt.

Through it all my belief in a higher power had to be
unyielding, unflinching, undaunted and unshakeable.
That is why I am still here, still standing and in my right mind.

THERE IS AN EAGLE IN YOU

Birds flock together but eagles fly alone. On your journey toward greatness you may Be required to take solo flight. Sometimes The people around you can be so limited in Their thinking that they cannot see where you are going. Their minds may not allow them to stretch that far. Don't let that stop you! Don't be afraid to go alone. Don't be afraid to go where no one has gone before. Like the eagles, you must be willing to take solo flight to reach new levels. Now stretch forth your wings and soar to your greatness! There is an eagle in you!

THE LITTLE THINGS

Sometimes we can get so weighed down
with our day to day lives that we forget
to stop and appreciate the little miracles
all around us. For example, the essence
of nature, the beauty of a flower, the wonder
of the sky. Observe all that surrounds you
today. Appreciate the beauty they possess
and recognize that you are at one with the
universe.

GREATNESS IS YOUR DESTINY

Greatness is your destiny, if you believe that it is. The possibilities for your life are unlimited. It starts with believing. We have all heard that saying, "seeing is believing." Someone once said, "believing is seeing." You must first be able to see what you want in your mind's eye before it can manifest into the physical world. Have you ever wondered why some people seem to have an abundance of everything good in life, while others struggle? When you genuinely believe that you are just as worthy, just as deserving, and just as capable as anyone else, your world will open up. It will open up to every possibility that was blocked by self-doubt and fear. Believe in yourself, be true to yourself, and most important of all, love yourself. Never stop working to make your dreams come true, and know in your heart that one day your dreams will come to pass. Everything is possible, if you just believe!

A NEW DAY

As the sun sets closing out each day
a new day is on the horizon. Each
day represents an opportunity to start
again. It is a chance to become better
than the day before. We cannot go
backward, only forward. Therefore,
we must learn from the past as we
prepare for the future. What did you
learn about yourself yesterday? How
will you use that information to become
a better person today? As you journey
out into the world, share the joy that is
you and make it a great day!

GIVE IT TO YOURSELF

When you need someone to love, love yourself.
When you need some attention, focus on you.
When you need to know that you are great, let yourself know.
When you need a present, buy it gift-wrapped.
When you need a night out on the town, just go.
When you need a pep talk, start talking.
When you need to hear that you are loved, tell yourself.
When you need something don't wait for someone else,
Give it to yourself!

IMAGINATION

My imagination is a place where I can go
to be who I want to be,
to see what I want to see,
to hear what I want to hear,
to feel what I want to feel.

With my imagination I can
see beauty that is boundless,
feel love that is priceless,
know joy that is endless,
live a life that is fearless.

With my imagination I want to
create my greatest fantasies,
express my innermost thoughts,
laugh until it hurts,
make my dreams come true.

With my imagination I can find
the peace that my heart has never felt,
the tranquility that I've never known,
the hope that was once lost,
the life that I was meant to live.

With my imagination I will
live in a world where my truth matters,
dwell in a place where my desires prevail,
exist in parts where I am compelled to laugh,
reside where every road leads to the right path.

With my imagination
the images will come alive,
dancing across the pages of my life,
as I give birth to dreams that were once out of sight,
and make myself believe everything will be all right.

PRETENDING ON A BAD DAY

This morning I gazed outside my window.
I had no place in particular to go.
I felt tired from a night that was rough.
I didn't know life could be so tough.

Raindrops were falling from the sky.
It was the perfect day to have a good cry.

I'm so full of fear that I'm shaking inside
With feelings that my face has been challenged to hide.
I feel like I can't show others this weak side of me,
Not when courageous and strong is all that I pretend to be.

When I'm all alone in the middle of the night
My mind is constantly engaged in a fight,
Rehashing every mistake I ever made,
Instead of allowing painful memories to fade.

Haunted by failures, problems and challenges,
Praying to God I can repair the damages.

Feeling weary as I drift off to sleep,
My bleeding heart continues to weep.

In the morning I will rise again
With many internal wounds to mend.

Pretending everything is all right,
Ignoring what happens in the middle of the night
Because I can't show others this weak side of me,
Not when courageous and strong is all that I pretend to be.

RARE

Sometimes I feel so alone
and there are people everywhere.
It's like no one understands me
because my thoughts are so rare.

My mind wanders to distant places
trying to make sense of the world.
I can spend countless hours daydreaming
the way I did when I was a girl.

I see a pretty blue bird
soaring through the sky.
As he fades into the distance
I ask myself why.

I feel the wind blowing my hair
and the sun beaming upon my face.
The beauty of nature surrounds me
in a world that is a mysterious place.

Part Seven
Love and Life

DREAM LOVE

Allow me to nurture you with my soft embrace
And place my sweet kisses upon your face.

I've already imaged your hands caressing my hips
And your smooth brown skin pressed against my lips.

Don't be afraid of this love that is strong.
The way we feel, what could possibly go wrong?

Your eyes speak volumes when you look at me.
The love you feel is plain to see.

I picture us sharing a life together.
Please say you want to be mine forever.

I want to build you up when the world brings you down.
I want to be a friend to you when no one else is around.

You can whisper your secrets in my ear,
The thoughts you don't want anyone else to hear.

I'll support your greatest hopes and dreams
And together we can become an awesome team.

I'll be your lover, counselor, confidant and friend
I'll be by your side until the very end.

AN UNKNOWN LOVE

I was going about my day
When a beauty caught my eye.
Why did this have to happen to me,
I'm feeling kind of shy.

Now his face invades my thoughts
Every night and day
And even though I love him
I wish he would go away.

I don't believe feeling like
This is good for any one.
Where has my common sense gone?
Suddenly I have none.

My thoughts are all over the place
And I'm not making any sense.
That's why I'm convinced it's not good
To have a love that's too intense.

I know that love can be beautiful
And so much more,
But if it's overpowering it can keep
You from the one whom you adore.

Thinking wild thoughts
While my heart is simply racing,
Sweaty palms, shaking hands,
This is a challenge I am facing.

This goes on every day
So it is really nothing new
A pair of passing eyes connect
and neither knows what to do.

Think of how many unknown loves
there must be scattered about the world.
Imagine how many times a boy
secretly falls in love with a girl.

Women have these feelings too
when they see that special man.
Maybe they kept quiet
or got that chilling feeling and ran.

There are unknown loves blooming
every day all across the land
but no one says anything because
the intensity is more than they can stand.

LOVE FROM A DISTANCE

When I look into your eyes I feel
the love pouring out of your heart.
I see the dreams of an inner child
on the verge of falling apart.

You want me but you
wonder if I want you.
You feel so confused and
you don't know what to do.

Should you risk heartbreak
and try to say hello?
Or should you protect your ego
and just let me go.

Either way there is a
high price to pay.
You decide you can't
make this decision today.

So for now you love
from a distance,
As you continue to fight
through your resistance.

You hope that in the end
true love will win
so that you'll never experience
such heartbreak again.

But in the end you lose,
all because you couldn't choose.
The love of your life is gone.
Now you sigh from morning till dawn,
Loving from a distance.

COULD THIS BE LOVE THIS TIME

I was nervous when I met, you then I looked into your eyes.
I relaxed when I saw that there was someone special inside.

All of my hopes and dreams for love suddenly came to mind
I thought, is this real and could this really be love this time?

Will we go for long romantic walks in the park?
Will we hold hands while gazing at the stars in the dark?

Will you teach me new things and inspire me to grow?
Will you pick me up when I am feeling low?

Will you be my strength when I am weak?
Will you be the protector that I seek?

Will you let me be everything to you?
Will you let me be the one you come running to?

Will I look at your faults and love you anyway?
Will I think that you are perfect in every way?

Will we walk down the aisle and say "I do"?
Will we make each other's dreams come true?

TRUE LOVE

Imagine feeling loved despite all mistakes,
Never feeling judgments or painful heartaches.

Whenever you need to talk to your friend,
He always has a little time to spend.

Imagine freely sharing your secrets with someone,
Knowing that your trust will never come undone.

When you experience success his heart feels glad,
And he cheers you up whenever you feel sad.

He wishes good things would happen to you,
Because the love you share couldn't be more true.

The trust you share will be there until the end,
Because you both understand the value of a friend.

EYES THAT SPEAK

Your eyes speak to me each time I look inside.
One glimpse takes me on your emotional ride.

When you are happy your eyes talk to me,
Sparkling with joy for all the world to see.

When you are not feeling well,
Your eyes have the story to tell.

They say, "I'm feeling bad today,"
Expressing things mere words can't say.

When you are up to something suspicious,
The slant in your eyes tells me if it's malicious.

Eyes truly are the windows to the soul,
They speak of stories untold.

If you want to know what someone is feeling,
Look in their eyes for something revealing.

OBSERVATION POINT

I took a walk in the park today,
Observing life in a whole new way.
I noticed things I hadn't seen before,
Appreciating the little things so much more

Like the warm summer breeze
Blowing gently against my skin,
And the leaves falling from the trees
Blowing aimlessly in the wind.

Like the fountain of water cascading
Down an artistic sculpture of man,
And the flowers so beautifully crafted
By nature's nurturing hands.

Like the clouds I saw in the sky
When I got lost in my own daydreams,
And the beauty of daylight that
Brightens the sky as the sun beams.

Like the free-flowing stream that caught
My attention as I casually passed by,
And the colorful birds that occasionally
Soar through the beautiful sky.

Today I discovered love and the world suddenly changed.
My senses have been heightened and my thoughts rearranged.
A true love more powerful than mere words could ever express,
It has opened up my heart and revealed to me life's best.

WHAT YOUR LOVE HAS DONE TO ME

Why are my feelings so dependent upon you?
If you have a good day, then I do too.

If you are unhappy and you let me know,
In an instant my feelings start to show.

Emotionally you take me wherever you go,
From your mountain highs to your valley lows,

It's as if my emotions are connected to you,
And I can no longer control what they do.

I experience your joy and I feel your pain,
But I love you so much I can't complain.

The first glimpse of your smile captured my heart,
And since that day I don't want to part.

I melt at the mere thought of your touch.
I never thought I could love someone so much.

Look what your love has done to me.
My life is more than I thought it could be.

Part Eight
Social Awareness

AT WAR

Take a look at what is going on around here,
A country is at war and terrorists have us living in fear.

Tell me what is the value of a life today.
It can't be much or we wouldn't kill this way.

Every day we see it all over the evening news.
Why does violence have to be the option we choose?

It seems men have such contempt for one another.
When will we learn to love our brother?

Slowly we have become desensitized,
To the point where empathy is no longer realized.

We can't risk becoming too emotionally involved.
Who knows how long the war will go unresolved?

Look at what happened in the Vietnam War,
A tragedy no one wants to talk about any more.

The Haitians and Africans fight all the time,
A typical response is, "It's no business of mine."

We have free will to do what is right,
Yet we still choose to argue and fight.

Constantly doing what we know is wrong.
We have been doing the same thing for far too long.

Why can't we find another way?
When all else fails, kneel down and pray.

The answer may not come right away,
But the truth will be revealed some day.

There has to be a purpose for all this,
Peaceful resolution is my prayer and my wish.

MAHOGANY SKIN

When I enter a room in my mahogany skin
I wonder what they think of me.
Do they see me for who I am
or is their vision tainted by who I am supposed to be?

It can be difficult to look this way
when you need a job and a place to stay.
No matter how much you love yourself
someone will judge you in a negative way.

The knife feels sharper and the wound cuts deeper
when inflicted by my own sister or brother.
The loyalty you expected but didn't get
creates a feeling comparable to no other.

We find so many ways to separate
but can we find a way to come together.
When are we going to implement solutions?
Because we can't live this way forever?

Light skin, dark skin,
that is one way to divide us all.
Rich man, poor man,
money can create a most divisive wall.

Well-known, unknown,
that's another way to play the division game.
Related, unrelated,
family and friend connections are another source to blame.

What if the only category to divide us
was good versus bad?
We would have a better chance at making it
than our ancestors had.

Funny how something so beautiful
can evoke such reactions in the hearts of man.
Because of this skin people have suffered
and died all across this great land.

Did you know when you have this skin
you are often the envy of man?
People may question you
but most fear what they don't understand.

Mahogany skin, rich in texture,
soft to the touch, and visually enticing.
Holding deep mysteries, unimaginable power
and provoking fear that is frightening.

ILLEGAL SUBSTANCE

Self-destruction at the hands of their own actions,
Triggering society to have a multitude of reactions.

Help them, love them, hate them, forget a lost cause.
Incarcerate them with the enforcement of unfair laws.

Why risk doing drugs for a temporary high?
Let's really try to understand the reasons why.

When I attempted to put myself in their shoes,
I entered the world of the lost and confused.

Why turn to something that will hurt you more in the end?
A battle with drugs is a fight you know you can't win.

To escape the pain of a reality most don't understand,
Some of which is created by a faulty perception of man.

Most of which is self-inflicted
By a mind and body that's so addicted.

Not only to the drugs and self-destruction
But to an ideology that began this corruption.

Subconsciously taught to be inferior,
Unconsciously acting out what's in the interior.

Trapped by a mindset that they can't seem to escape,
Where freedom is on the other side of their mind's closed gate.

Depression, repression, oppression, resulting in aggression,
What a lesson for the mind leaving a lasting impression.

Understanding this phenomenon does not make it right
But it does make it easier to understand an addict's plight.

EVERYBODY IS SOMEBODY

In our world where little praise
is given to those who are without,
So many look up to those
with money, power and clout.

In our world we are separated
by the haves and have nots,
There are those who have a little
and those who have a lot.

In our world we often ignore
people who don't seem to measure up
And then we wonder why so
many young minds are corrupt.

In our world worth is often dependent
upon kinship, fortune or fame.
Our desire to increase our
self-worth is the source to blame.

One's worth should not
be measured superficially,
Instead it should be
measured substantially.

Everybody is somebody
no matter where they are in their existence.
Even those who aren't doing well
in a life marked by inconsistence.

Everybody is somebody
even if nobody knows your name.
God created us in his image so
on some level we are all the same.

Everybody is somebody
although your voice may seem faint.
That will change when you speak
out and remove your own restraints.

Everybody is somebody,
what a powerful message to send.
It's not how you start the race
but how you finish in the end.

THROUGH THE EYES OF A CHILD

Through the eyes of a child
how enormous the world must seem,
so many unanswered questions
so much of life yet unseen.

With so many new things
to learn and explore,
each day presents a child
with adventures galore.

Living for today because
tomorrow is so far away,
allowing their impulses to
guide them through each day.

Innocent to the evil that
looms throughout the universe,
they are soon taught to avoid
strangers for fear of the worse.

In need of guidance that
adults so often fail to give,
longing for the love we all
crave to be happy and live.

Dreaming thoughts
that are unrealistic,
asking questions and
wanting specifics.

Through the eyes of a child
the world can be a scary place.
It is up to the adults to keep them
secure, sound and safe.

YESTERDAY, TODAY AND TOMORROW

Yesterday is gone forever
and will never come again.
We can't change the past and
broken hearts take time to mend.

If something went wrong
we can learn from the mistake,
and then we must let it go
for our own mind's sake.

Today is here now but
soon it will be yesterday.
A part of the past that
will be forever gone away.

Tomorrow is coming but
it won't be here for long.
Learn from your mistakes
if anything should go wrong.

The days seem to go
by faster and faster,
forcing us to search for time
to experience joy and laughter.

That is why we cannot waste
Time rehashing old mistakes.
It's part of life to experience
Disappointment and heartache.

From negative experiences
we can become stronger.
Over time your disappointments
won't hurt any longer.

Yesterday, today and tomorrow
they come and go so fast.
Plan for the future, live in the
present and learn from the past.

THE POWER OF ONE

What kind of difference can one person make?
A question many of us have asked ourselves
When faced with the opportunity to affect change.

What kind of difference can one person make?
It's like throwing a pebble in the ocean
To make a quiet ripple against a roaring wave.

What kind of difference can one person make?
It's like thinking your one vote in an election
Could actually affect the outcome of the race.

What kind of difference can one person make?
It's like trying to solve a world full of problems
When you can only reach people one by one.

The power of one can create the momentum to move mountains.
All it takes is one person with the heart to step out,
Serving as a leader for others to eagerly follow.

The power of one can make the difference
When others feel the same way you feel
But lack the courage and conviction to speak up.

The power of one can be the deciding factor
In a life or death situation where one must make a
Swift decision about the best course of action.

The power of one can change the world as so many have,
Jesus Christ, Nelson Mandela, Mohandas Ghandi,
Mother Theresa, Harriet Tubman, John F. Kennedy,
Medger Evers, Rosa Parks, Malcom X, Muhammad
Ali, Martin Luther King, Jr....